Which. is Which?

by
Josephine Croser

CONTENTS

About this book 3
Which is Which? 4
Crocodile or Alligator? 6
Rabbit or Hare? 7
Earwig or Scorpion? 8
Honey Bee or Paper Wasp? 9
Butterfly or Moth? 10
Dolphin or Porpoise? 11
Monkey or Ape? 12
Frog or Toad? 13
Octopus or Squid? 14
Emu or Ostrich? 15
Did you know? 16
Answers 17
How to play 'Which is it?' 17
The 'Which is it?' game .... back cover

ABOUT THIS BOOK

This book is about animals that
look like each other.
For example, do *you* know the
difference between a crocodile
and an alligator?

This book will help you to know
which is **which.**

WHICH IS WHICH?

 crocodile
or
alligator?

A

B

 rabbit
or
hare?

A

B

 earwig
or
scorpion?

A

B

 honey
bee or
paper
wasp?

A

B

 butterfly
or
moth?

A

B

4

WHICH IS WHICH?

porpoise
or
dolphin?

A   B

monkey
or
ape?

A   B

frog
or
toad?

A   B

octopus
or
squid?

A   B

ostrich
or
emu?

A   B

5

CROCODILE OR ALLIGATOR?

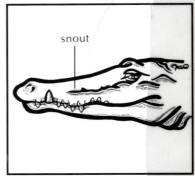

Crocodile

Most crocodiles have a narrow snout. One longer tooth on each side of the lower jaw can be seen sticking up when the jaws are closed.

Alligator

Alligators have a broad snout. The longer teeth on the lower jaw cannot be seen when the jaws are closed.

Rabbit

Rabbits have a furry body, long ears, a short up-turned tail, short front legs and long hind-legs.

Hare

Hares have a similar body shape to that of the rabbit but they are bigger and stronger. Hares have longer hind-legs and ears than rabbits do.

EARWIG OR SCORPION?

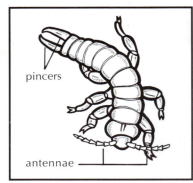

pincers

antennae

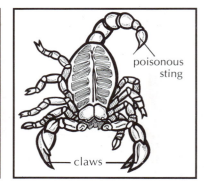

poisonous
sting

claws

Earwig

Earwigs have six legs, two antennae and a strong pair of pincers. They do not have a sting or claws.

Scorpion

Scorpions have eight legs and a poisonous sting in the tail. Scorpions do not have antennae. They use two large pairs of claws for holding prey.

HONEY BEE OR PAPER WASP?

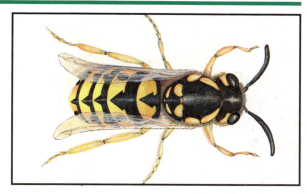

Honey Bee

Honey bees collect pollen and carry it in a basket of stiff hairs on each hind-leg. When they rest, their wings are flat.

Paper Wasp

Paper wasps do not have a basket of stiff hairs and do not collect pollen. When they rest, their wings are folded back and look narrower than a bee's wings.

BUTTERFLY OR MOTH?

Butterfly

Butterflies have two thin antennae with a knob at the end. When they rest, they usually hold their wings upright. Butterfly caterpillars do not make cocoons. They just turn into pupae.

Moth

Moths have two wide antennae, often shaped like feathers. When moths rest, many hold their wings out to the side. Most moth caterpillars spin cocoons before turning into pupae.

DOLPHIN OR PORPOISE?

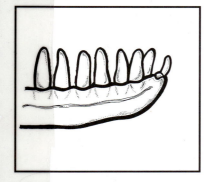

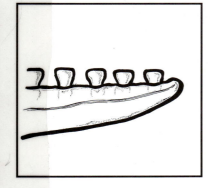

Dolphin

Dolphins have a snout shaped like a beak, and pointed teeth. They often jump out of the water. The fin on the back of the dolphin is usually curved.

Porpoise

Porpoises have a blunt, rounded snout and flat, spade-shaped teeth. They hardly ever jump out of the water. Most porpoises have a trian-gular fin on their back.

MONKEY OR APE?

Monkey

Most monkeys have a tail. Their arms are the same length or shorter than their legs. They walk on their feet and the palms of their hands.

Ape

Apes do not have a tail. Their arms are longer than their legs. Most apes walk on their feet and the knuckles of their hands.

Frog

Frogs have shiny, smooth skin. Their bodies and legs are usually long and slender.

Toad

Toads have dull, wrinkly skin with lumps called *warts*. Their bodies and legs are usually short and stubby.

OCTOPUS OR SQUID?

Octopus

Octopuses have eight long arms which are all the same length. Their bodies are like flattened spheres.

Squid

Squid have ten arms. Eight are short and two are long. Squid have long, oval-shaped bodies.

Emu

Emus are grey-brown. They have three toes on each foot. Emus lay dark green eggs.

Ostrich

The male ostrich is black and white but the female is brown. They have two toes on each foot. Ostriches lay white eggs.

DID YOU KNOW?

Crocodiles live in both salt and fresh water, but **alligators** only live in fresh water.

Rabbits raise their young in burrows, whereas **hares** raise their young in nests on the ground.

Earwigs usually live in groups, however **scorpions** live alone. Sometimes the female scorpion attacks and eats the male after mating.

Honey bees can sting only once and then they die, while **paper wasps** can sting many times and do not die after stinging.

Butterflies fly by day, but **moths** usually fly by night.

Dolphins often adapt to captivity, whereas **porpoises** usually do not survive in captivity.

Apes use their arms to swing along under branches, whereas **monkeys** walk along branches and some can use their tail to grip.